THE THREE PREDATEERS

Donald Gorbach

ISBN-10 1979687560
ISBN-13 978-1979687560

"WHAT I LEARNED LATER IN LIFE, TOO LATE, IS THAT
WHEN YOU HAVE POWER OVER ANOTHER PERSON,
ASKING THEM TO LOOK AT YOUR D--K ISN'T A
QUESTION. IT'S A PREDICAMENT FOR THEM."

— LOUIS C.K.

www.ingramcontent.com/pod-product-compliance
Lightning Source LLC
Chambersburg PA
CBHW050912260726
48660CB00001B/154